ANCIENT AND MEDIEVAL PEOPLE

The Roman Gladiators

Louise Park
and Timothy Love

Marshall Cavendish
Benchmark

New York

This edition first published in 2010 in the United States of America by Marshall Cavendish Benchmark.

Marshall Cavendish Benchmark
99 White Plains Road
Tarrytown, NY 10591
www.marshallcavendish.us

First published in 2009 by
MACMILLAN EDUCATION AUSTRALIA PTY LTD
15–19 Claremont Street, South Yarra 3141

Visit our website at www.macmillan.com.au or go directly to www.macmillanlibrary.com.au

Associated companies and representatives throughout the world.

Library of Congress Cataloging-in-Publication Data

Park, Louise, 1961—
    The Roman gladiators / by Louise Park and Timothy Love.
       p. cm. – (Ancient and medieval people)
    ISBN 978-0-7614-4443-5
    1. Gladiators–Rome–Juvenile literature. 2. Rome–Social life and customs–Juvenile literature. 3.
    Rome–History–Juvenile literature. I. Love, Timothy. II. Title.
    GV35.P37 2009
    796'.0937–dc22
                        2008055775

Edited by Julia Carlomagno
Text and cover design by Cristina Neri, Canary Graphic Design
Page layout by Cristina Neri, Canary Graphic Design
Photo research by Legend Images
Illustrations by Colby Heppéll, Giovanni Caselli, and Paul Konye

Printed in the United States

Acknowledgments
The author and the publisher are grateful to the following for permission to reproduce
copyright material:

Front cover photo: Roman colosseum © Alexandr Tkachuk/iStockphoto; parchment © Selahattin
BAYRAM/iStockphoto

Photos courtesy of: Background photos throughout: old paper © peter zelei/iStockphoto; mosaic tiles
© Hedda Gjerpen/iStockphoto; Roman column © PhotographerOlympus/iStockphoto; Roman figures
© A-Digit/iStockphoto; Coo-ee Historical Picture Library, **14**, **30**; Roman/Getty Images, **19**; Giovanni
Caselli's Universal Library Unlimited, **11**, **18**, **22**, **25**, **26**, **27**, **28**; © Alexandr Tkachuk/iStockphoto,
4 (colosseum); Dreamworks/Universal/The Kobal Collection/Buitendijk, Jaap, **6**; Photolibrary ©
PhotoBliss/Alamy, **24**; Photolibrary © Photos 12/Alamy, **21**; Photolibrary/Ann Ronan Pictures, **8**;
Photolibrary/Christian Kober, **15**; Photolibrary/Mary Evans Picture Library, **29**; Photolibrary/The Print
Collector, **7**; © Denis Babenko/Shutterstock, **20**.

Sources for quotes used in text: Quote from the Roman philosopher Seneca, **27**.

While every care has been taken to trace and acknowledge copyright, the publisher tenders
their apologies for any accidental infringement where copyright has proved untraceable.
Where the attempt has been unsuccessful, the publisher welcomes information that would redress the
situation.

The authors and publisher wish to advise that to the best of their ability they have tried to verify
dates, facts, and the spelling of personal names and terminology. The accuracy and reliability of some
information on ancient civilizations is difficult in instances where detailed records were not kept or did
not survive.

Contents

Glossary Words

When a word is printed in **bold**, you can look up its meaning in the Glossary on page 31.

Who Were the Roman Gladiators?

The Roman gladiators were trained fighters who performed for huge crowds in **amphitheaters** throughout the Roman Empire. Gladiators fought both each other and wild animals, sometimes to death.

The Roman Empire

The Roman Empire extended through Europe and parts of the Mediterranean and Africa. It is believed to have begun around 27 BCE and to have lasted until around 395 BCE. The Roman Empire was ruled by an **Emperor** and governed by a **senate**, both based in Rome.

WHAT'S IN A NAME?

Gladiator

The name *gladiator* comes from the Latin word *gladiatores*. It means "one who uses a sword".

Roman Gladiators Timeline

264 BCE
First recorded gladiatorial games are held in Rome

202 BCE
One of the earliest gladiatorial games, which included dangerous animals

80 BCE
The first amphitheater is constructed in Pompeii

46 BCE
Julius Caesar holds a sea battle and three thousand gladiators participate

2 BCE
Emperor Augustus holds a sea battle and six thousand gladiators participate

59 CE
Emperor Nero bans gladiatorial games in Pompeii for ten years, following a slave riot

70 CE
Work begins on the **Colosseum**

200 BCE   100 BCE   0 CE   100 CE

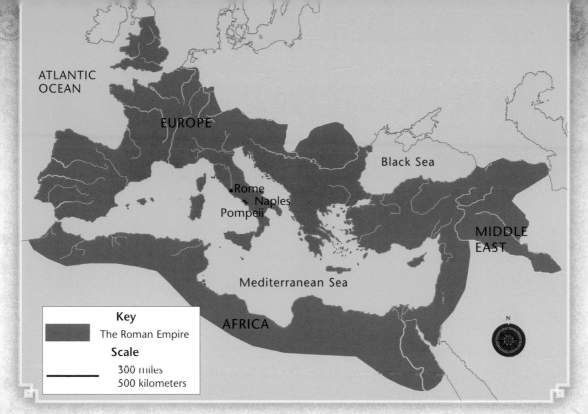

ATLANTIC
OCEAN

EUROPE

Black Sea

•Rome
Naples
Pompeii

MIDDLE
EAST

Mediterranean Sea

AFRICA

Key
The Roman Empire
Scale
300 miles
500 kilometers

N

The Roman Empire
stretched across
the continents of
Europe and Africa.

The Formation of the Roman Gladiators

Roman gladiators formed during the early periods of the Roman Empire. Gladiators were mostly slaves, criminals, or prisoners of war who were forced to go to gladiator schools. Sometimes these slaves were sold to gladiator owners, who forced them to train and fight. As the gladiatorial games grew, so did the number of **volunteer gladiators**. Volunteer gladiators often were poor men attracted by the chance to become famous and earn some money.

Quick Facts

When Did the Gladiatorial Games Take Place?
The gladiatorial games took place for more than six hundred years to entertain those in the Roman Empire.

❖ Rome's first recorded gladiatorial games took place in 264 BCE, in honor of the death of a Roman called Brutus Pera. The games used three pairs of slaves as gladiators.

❖ The gladiatorial games were officially abolished by Emperor Honorius in 404 CE, six hundred years after they began.

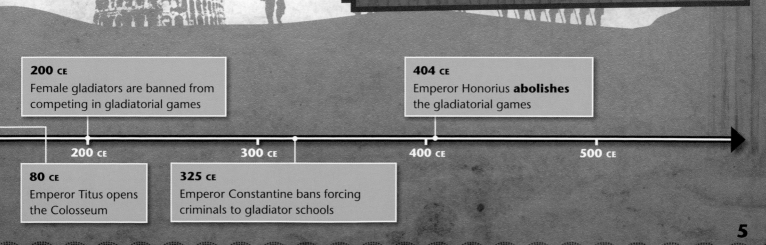

200 CE
Female gladiators are banned from competing in gladiatorial games

404 CE
Emperor Honorius **abolishes** the gladiatorial games

200 CE   300 CE   400 CE   500 CE

80 CE
Emperor Titus opens the Colosseum

325 CE
Emperor Constantine bans forcing criminals to gladiator schools

The Development of the Gladiatorial Games

The gladiatorial games were popular among the Roman **elite** as well as among ordinary citizens. Over time, they became the most popular form of entertainment in Rome.

The Origin of the Games

It was once believed that the gladiatorial games may have come from the **Etruscans**, who killed prisoners at the funerals of important people because they believed it kept spirits away. Many historians now believe that the idea of gladiators came from Greece. The Ancient Greeks held fights, contests, games, and sacrifices at their funerals.

The Development of the Games

In the film Gladiator, Maximus (played by Russell Crowe, right) fights in gladiatorial games.

The first gladiatorial games took place at the funerals of important Roman officials. Some believed that one gladiator killing another at a funeral would please the many gods that the Ancient Romans worshipped. Soon every official in Rome was planning bigger and better events for their own funerals. Musicians even played during the fights, matching the **tempo** of their music to the pace of the combat.

The Political Role of the Games

Over time the gladiatorial games came to play an important political function. Politicians in the senate needed votes to keep their positions. Many politicians discovered that the citizens' desire for gladiatorial games could help them to win votes. The Emperor also learned that holding gladiatorial games was the best way to keep power and stay popular.

Quick Facts

What Were the Largest Planned Gladiatorial Games?

There were several large planned gladiatorial games during the Roman Empire, some involving thousands of gladiators.

❖ The largest gladiatorial games were held by Emperor Trajan in 107 CE. They involved five thousand pairs of gladiators.

❖ General Titus Flaminius held gladiatorial games to mark the death of his father. The games lasted three days and involved seventy-four gladiators.

❖ Julius Caesar planned to hold 320 gladiator fights at his daughter's funeral. However, the senate stopped him by ruling that there had to be a limit on the amount of money that could be spent on gladiatorial games.

Training to Become a Gladiator

Slaves, prisoners, and volunteers trained to be gladiators in gladiator schools. Life in gladiator schools was often harsh and difficult.

Gladiator Schools

Gladiator schools were found all over the Roman Empire. Some historians estimate that there were more than one hundred gladiator schools. The men who owned these schools were called *lanistae*, and they were often former gladiators who had won their **freedom**. These *lanistae* often visited slave markets and bought slaves to train as gladiators.

Life in a Gladiator School

Gladiators lived harsh lives in gladiator schools. They slept in tiny, dark cells within **barracks**, where they were constantly guarded. A gladiator's typical diet consisted of grains, beans, oatmeal, and barley. It was believed that eating these foods would stop gladiators from bleeding to death.

Gladiators trained in the same groups every day. Training involved learning a series of routines. These routines were broken into various acts or scenes, similar to a play. Gladiators were even trained to die in a way that would satisfy the audience.

Lanistae (who, unlike gladiators, wore robes) trained gladiators to fight in gladiator schools.

A gladiator took an oath to the gods when he first joined a gladiator school.

Taking Oaths and Signing Contracts

Each gladiator had to take the gladiator's oath, known as the *sacramentum gladiatorium*. Taking the oath meant agreeing to be treated as a slave without **civil rights**. It also meant suffering social disgrace, or being seen as the lowest members of society. The oath was, "I will endure to be burned, to be bound, to be beaten, and to be killed by the sword," and it was made to the gods.

Gladiators also signed contracts with the *lanistae*. These contracts covered:

❖ how often gladiators were to perform

❖ what weapons they would use

❖ how much money they would earn for a fight

❖ what medical care they would receive and what living conditions would be like

Quick Facts

What Were the Most Famous Gladiator Schools?

The most famous gladiator schools were found in Italy.

❖ Two well-known gladiator schools were Capula, which was near Naples, and the Pompeii Gladiator Barracks in Pompeii.

❖ The most important school in Rome was the Ludus Magnus. It was connected to the Colosseum by an underground tunnel.

❖ The Ludus Matutinus, in Rome, was a famous school where gladiators learned to fight against animals.

SPOTLIGHT ON
the Ludus Magnus

Spotlight On

WHAT: The Ludus Magnus

ALSO KNOWN AS: Rome's most famous gladiator school

BUILT BY: Emperor Domitian

The Ludus Magnus was the largest and most **prestigious** gladiator school in Rome. It had two levels built around a large **arena**, in which gladiators trained and exercised. At least three thousand seats were built in the arena for **spectators** to watch the gladiators training.

The Ludus Magnus also had about 130 cells where gladiators slept under guard. The cells were grouped into four wings.

The school closed when gladiator performances were abolished by Emperor Honorius in 404 CE. Its ruins were discovered in 1937, and **excavations** continued until 1957.

Many gladiators learned to fight at the Ludus Magnus.

Ruins of the Ludus Magnus consist of almost half the arena and about half of the gladiator cells on the bottom level.

Tunnel to the Colosseum

The Ludus Magnus was connected to the Colosseum by an underground tunnel. The tunnel began under the Colosseum and emerged in the southwest corner of the Ludus Magnus. The entrance to the tunnel was 7 feet (2.17 meters) wide.

What You Should Know About...

The Ludus Magnus

❖ Some spectator entrances were reserved for important people. An entrance located at the center of the building on the northern side held a special seat, or place of honor.

❖ A marble blueprint of the Ludus magnus was found among the building plans for the city of Rome. It shows the layout of the school, including the tunnel that connected it to the Colosseum. The marble city plans hung on a wall in the **Forum** during the Roman Empire.

Types of Gladiators

Many different types of gladiators fought in gladiatorial games. Some types of gladiators fought other types of gladiators, and even wild animals. Some types of gladiators fought each other.

Bestiarii fought large, dangerous animals, such as lions and tigers. They were often killed by these animals.

Retiarii aimed to knock out their opponents with a **trident** and trap them with a net. They fought without helmets.

Andabatae rode on horseback, charging at each other like knights in a medieval **joust**.

Secutores fought against retiarii gladiators. Their helmets were smooth so that they did not get caught in the retiarii nets.

Gladiators Who Fought Each Other

Retiarii and secutores gladiators usually fought against each other, while murmillone, thraeces, and hoplomachi gladiators sometimes fought each other.

Murmillone carried a sword and a rectangular shield, and wore a helmet with a fish on the **crest**.

Essedarii rode **chariots**. During battle, essedarii would try to break their **opponents**' chariot. Their battles often ended with sword fights on foot.

Thraeces wore broad helmets and carried curved swords, which could reach around their opponents' shields.

Dimachaeri did not wear armor or protective clothing. They carried two daggers but did not carry shields.

Hoplomachi were based on Spartan hoplite soldiers, and they wore full body armor.

Gladiator Weapons and Armor

As gladiatorial games became more popular, different types of weapons and armor were developed. Gladiators used different weapons and wore different armor to suit their fighting styles.

Weapons

Gladiator weapons included swords, lances, nets, and bows.

❖ Two common types of sword were the Thracian sica and the Acinace. The Thracian sica was a curved sword used by thraeces gladiators. The Acinace was a single-edged sword used by dimachaeri gladiators.

❖ Three common types of lance were the trident, the hasta, and the pilum. The trident was a spear with three prongs used by retiarii gladiators. The hasta was a long pole used by essedarii gladiators. The pilum was a **javelin** with a long, metal point used by several types of gladiators.

❖ Two common types of net were the laquesus missilis and the rete. The laquesus missilis was a lasso made out of leather or strong rope and was used by laquerarius gladiators. The rete was a net made from strong rope with blades or weights attached to its edges. It was used by retiarii gladiators.

❖ The arcus et Sagitiae was a bow used to shoot opponents during special gladiatorial games. It was used by several types of gladiators.

Retiarii gladiators carried tridents to knock out opponents, and nets to trap and wound them.

Armor

Armor worn by gladiators included breastplates, manicas, cataphractes, and helmets.

- ❖ Breastplates were often made of bronze and were worn to protect the torso.
- ❖ Manicas were made of leather and were worn to protect the arms.
- ❖ Cataphractes were fabric tunics with small leather or metal scales sewn onto them.
- ❖ Helmets were metal or leather. Metal helmets offered more protection, but they were heavier than leather helmets.

Some gladiators also wore leather shin guards and belts.

Shields

Most gladiators carried shields to protect themselves during battle. Large body shields, called *scutum*, were rectangular or oval. Smaller defensive shields, called *clypeus*, were round or oval. Wooden shields, called *parma*, were always round.

This man is dressed as a hoplomachi gladiator and is wearing a bronze breastplate and a metal helmet.

15

IN PROFILE: Flamma

In Profile

WHO: Flamma

NICKNAME: Loach

TYPE OF GLADIATOR: Secutor

DIED: Age thirty years, in his thirty-fourth fight

Flamma was one of the most famous and successful gladiators of his time. He performed in thirty-four gladiatorial games during his lifetime.

Flamma came from Syria, and it is thought that he was once a soldier in a private army. Some historians believe that he was condemned to become a gladiator for **insubordination**.

During his career as a gladiator, Flamma won twenty-one fights. He became so popular that sculptors made statues of him. His head was even used on a Roman coin.

Notable Moment

A gladiator's ultimate reward was freedom from fighting as a gladiator. Gladiators who survived three to five years of battle or won five fights could earn their freedom. Flamma was awarded his freedom four times but chose to remain a gladiator.

WHAT'S IN A NAME?

Rudis

The act of earning freedom was called *rudis*. The symbol of rudis was a wooden sword.

Flamma fought in the Colosseum in Rome.

Flamma's Gladiator Record

Not many records were kept of gladiators who fought in the gladiatorial games. Flamma's achievements, however, were recorded on his gravestone.

FLAMMA
'LOACH'

SECUTOR GLADIATOR

LIVED TO THIRTY YEARS OLD

FOUGHT THIRTY-FOUR TIMES

WON TWENTY-ONE TIMES

DREW NINE TIMES

WAS DEFEATED FOUR TIMES

What You Should Know About...

Flamma

❖ Flamma was a secutor gladiator, so he fought with a shield, a dagger, and a smooth helmet. most of his fights were against retiarii gladiators who fought with tridents and nets.

❖ It is believed that Flamma trained at the Ludus magnus.

❖ Flamma was so popular with the crowd that even when he lost, the Emperor would spare his life so that he could continue fighting.

Roman Amphitheaters

As the number of spectators at gladiatorial games grew, it became difficult to hold the games in open-air arenas, markets, or forums. Ancient Romans designed special buildings, called amphitheaters, to hold the games. Each amphitheater contained an arena, in which gladiators fought one another.

Roman amphitheaters were packed with spectators during gladiatorial games.

WHAT'S IN A NAME?

Arena

The word *arena* means sand. A thick layer of sand was laid down in arenas to soak up the blood from injured gladiators and animals.

Amphitheater

The word *amphitheater* comes from the Latin word *ampitheatrum*, which means "having seats on all sides." These seats often surrounded the arena in an oval shape known as an ellipse.

Building Amphitheaters

Amphitheaters were built because they could seat large audiences. Each amphitheater had many levels of seating that went all the way around the arena. As Roman amphitheaters were not carved into hills as Greek theaters were, they could be built almost anywhere.

The first amphitheater in Ancient Rome was the Circus Maximus. It could seat 25,000 spectators, and many gladiatorial games were held there during the Roman Empire. Other events, such as chariot races, foot races, boxing, and wrestling, were also held there.

Types of Amphitheaters

The first Roman amphitheaters were wooden, but they were quickly replaced by stone amphitheaters. Wooden amphitheaters sometimes caught fire or collapsed, whereas stone amphitheaters could handle all weather conditions. Today, the ruins of more than 220 stone amphitheaters are scattered across countries that were once part of the Roman Empire.

The first known stone amphitheater was built in Pompeii around 80 BCE. It could seat about 20,000 people. In 70 CE, the Romans began building a stone amphitheater that was designed to be bigger and better than all others. It became known as the Colosseum, and it could seat around 50,000 spectators.

Seating Arrangements

Before the rule of Emperor Augustus, there were no official rules about where citizens sat in amphitheaters. Emperor Augustus issued a **decree** to ensure that the first row of seats was always given to senators. He also set aside special seating for male citizens such as married men and young boys, who had a higher status than women, and he separated soldiers from ordinary citizens.

SPOTLIGHT ON
the Colosseum

── Spotlight On ──

WHAT: The Colosseum
ORIGINAL NAME: Amphitheatrum Flavium
WHERE: Rome
BUILT: 72–83 CE

The Colosseum was the most spectacular amphitheater of its time. It took between 20,000 and 30,000 slaves, engineers, and skilled workers more than ten years to complete, and when it was finished it was opened by Emperor Titus.

The amphitheater was 160 ft (49 m) high, 617 ft (188 m) long and 512 ft (156 m) wide. It had about eighty entrances for spectators. Four of these entrances were reserved for the Emperor, his family, and other important people.

Seating was spread over four levels, reaching 98 ft (30 m) high. The upper storey held the lower **social classes** and most women, while the lowest storey, which had the best view, was reserved for the most important citizen, such as married men and soldiers. Their seats were made from marble.

Quick Facts

Was the Colosseum Ever Damaged?

The Colosseum was damaged by fire and an earthquake.

❖ The damage sustained by fire took twenty years to repair.

❖ The southern side was destroyed by an earthquake. Some of the materials were **salvaged** and used in other buildings, such as St Peter's Basilica.

The Colosseum was built from concrete, marble, brick, and stone, so it has lasted for thousands of years.

Armed guards are believed to have lined the tunnel between the Ludus Magnus and the Colosseum, in order to make sure that gladiators entered the arena safely.

Tunnels

The Colosseum had many tunnels that connected it to surrounding buildings. The north-east tunnel connected the Colosseum to the Ludus Magnus. Gladiators used this tunnel to make a dramatic entrance into the arena. The tunnel was believed to be known as the gate of life because only the winning gladiators traveled back through it to the Ludus Magnus. The Colosseum had another tunnel known as the gate of death. Gladiators who were killed in battle were believed to have been dragged through this gate.

What You Should Know About...

The Colosseum

❖ To celebrate the opening of the Colosseum, Emperor Titan held a one-hundred-day festival of games. These games included gladiator fights and animal spectacles. more than nine thousand animals were killed during these performances.

❖ The Colosseum had an enormous **awning** that protected spectators from the sun. It took about one thousand men to put up the awning.

❖ There were many cages of wild animals beneath the Colosseum. These cages could be raised so that animals could appear in the middle of the arena.

Emperor Gladiators

Although gladiators were considered the lowest members of society, if they were successful they often won fame and respect. Emperors hungry for fame were known to fight as gladiators.

Which Emperors Fought?

Emperors who fought gladiators include:

- Caligula
- Lucius Verus
- Didius
- Commodus
- Nero
- Hadrian

Fixed Fights

Generally fights between gladiators and emperors were fixed so that emperors would be protected from harm. It is believed that many emperors fought knowing that they would not be killed or seriously injured. Emperors could choose their opponents and set the limits of the fight. In addition, most games between emperors and gladiators were performed using wooden swords, which would not cause serious injury.

Emperor Caligula fought as a gladiator to win fame and respect from the Roman people.

Emperor Caligula and Emperor Commodus

Emperor Caligula and Emperor Commodus used the arena to demonstrate their power and authority over gladiators and spectators.

❖ Both emperors demanded that ordinary citizens enter the arena and fight as gladiators.

❖ Roman historians reported a fight in which Emperor Caligula killed a gladiator by producing a real sword and stabbing his opponent to death. Caligula also had the awning removed from the Colosseum on an extremely hot day. He refused to let any spectator leave the Colosseum, in order to see the crowd suffer.

❖ Emperor Commodus is believed to have slaughtered thousands of bears, tigers, and other wild animals. While most gladiators fought against these animals to save their lives, Commodus often killed the animals when there was no threat to his life.

Emperor Commodus fought wild animals such as bears in order to impress spectators.

IN PROFILE:
Emperor Commodus

Emperor Commodus ruled the Roman Empire between 180 CE and 192 CE, and was considered a **tyrant**.

Commodus thrived on public performance and participated in more than 735 gladiatorial games. He fought as a secutor gladiator dressed like Hercules, and carried a lion's club and hide. He would **emulate** Hercules's triumphs by fighting wild animals. When Commodus fought against other gladiators he would win easily because fights were always fixed in his favor.

Many people plotted to take Commodus's life, due to his poor leadership and cruelty. His sister and cousin were involved in a failed plot to **assassinate** him. He was eventually poisoned and **strangled** to death in his bath.

Cruel Moments

Commodus became known for his cruelty and vanity in the arena. It was reported that he often went into battle with a real sword, while his opponent had only a wooden sword. He also slaughtered many helpless animals. At one event it was said that he killed one hundred bears.

Emperor Commodus Timeline

150 CE	160 CE	170 CE
161 CE Born to the emperor Marcus Aurelius	**166 CE** Made junior emperor at age five	**177 CE** Made joint emperor with Marcus Aurelius at age sixteen

Political Leadership

Commodus's desire for fame can also be seen in his political leadership as emperor. After rebuilding a part of Rome that was damaged by fire, he tried to rename the city "Colonia Commodiana," which means *city of Commodus.* He also tried to rename the Roman army and the senate after himself. Following the rebuilding of Rome, Commodus announced that he would take on extra duties in 193 CE. To celebrate this occasion, he planned to march from the Ludus Magnus to the senate dressed as a gladiator. However, he never made this march as he was assassinated in 192 CE.

What You Should Know About...

Emperor Commodus

❖ Commodus had statues **inscribed** with his achievements. One statue claimed that he killed 12,000 men.

❖ Commodus was said to be jealous of successful gladiators. It is believed that he had a gladiator called Julius Alexander executed because he had killed a lion with a javelin while on horseback.

❖ Commodus charged the city of Rome large amounts of money to see him perform. For every performance he charged one million sesterces, which were extremely valuable coins. Over time these payments damaged Rome's economy.

180 CE   190 CE   200 CE

180 CE
Becomes the sole emperor when Marcus Aurelius dies

192 CE
Assassinated while taking a bath

Attitudes Toward the Gladiatorial Games

While most citizens in the Roman Empire enjoyed gladiatorial games, some emperors and philosophers did not support this violent form of entertainment.

Emperors Who Took a Stand

Many emperors took a stand against the bloodshed and violence of the games. It is believed that Emperor Marcus Aurelius did not enjoy gladiatorial games very much. However, he did see the gladiators as superior athletes. In order to prevent bloodshed, he decreed that gladiator swords had to have blunt points, and he banned iron blades from the arena. Emperor Severus banned female gladiators from fighting in 200 CE. Emperor Constantine stopped gladiatorial games from being held in 325 CE and, in 404 CE, Emperor Honorius officially abolished the games.

Although the games were disliked by some emperors, they were popular with spectators, who would fill the Colosseum.

A Philosopher Who Spoke Out

The Roman philosopher Seneca was one of the few philosophers who spoke out against the gladiatorial games. He wrote of his distaste for the games during the reign of Emperor Caligula.

There is nothing so ruinous to good character as to idle away one's time at some spectacle. Vices have a way of creeping in because of the feeling of pleasure that it brings. Why do you think that I say that I personally return from shows greedier, more ambitious, and more given to luxury, and I might add, with thoughts of greater cruelty and less humanity, simply because I have been among humans?

—THE ROMAN PHILOSOPHER SENECA

Quick Facts

Did Gladiators Ever Protest Against the Gladiatorial Games?

Gladiators such as Spartacus protested against the gladiatorial games.

❖ Three slave **revolts** occurred during the period when the games were held. These revolts were known as the Servile wars.

❖ The largest of these revolts was led by the gladiator Spartacus.

Some protesters ran out into the arena to try to stop gladiators from killing each other.

IN PROFILE: Spartacus

In Profile

WHO: Spartacus
TYPE OF GLADIATOR: Thracian
BORN: 109 BCE
DIED: 71 BCE

Spartacus lived in Thrace, Greece, until he left home to join the Roman army. Later, he **deserted** the army and was captured and sold into slavery. Eventually, he was sent to a gladiator school in the city of Capula.

Spartacus led a large slave revolt in Capula. At the height of the revolt Spartacus had gathered about 120,000 followers to support him. Spartacus became a hero not just for his fighting ability but for his cleverness in battle and his qualities as a leader.

Spartacus and the other **rebel** slaves were defeated in a major battle in southern Italy. It is believed that Spartacus died in this battle.

Notable Moment

In 73 BCE Spartacus initiated a slave revolt to fight for freedom. Spartacus and his chief aide, Crixus, escaped from Capula with seventy to eighty other gladiators, and carts filled with weapons. They set up camp at the top of Mount Vesuvius, where they were joined by more slaves.

Spartacus Timeline

110 BCE **100 BCE** **90 BCE**

109 BCE
Born in Thrace, Greece

73 BCE
Leads the gladiator revolt at Capula

Spartacus died in a battle in southern Italy, and the slave revolt was defeated soon afterward.

Defeating Enemies

The senate sent **legions** of three thousand soldiers to capture or kill Spartacus and the rebel slaves, but Spartacus defeated them. The soldiers aimed to attack Spartacus and the other slaves at the top of Mount Vesuvius, believing that they would be trapped there. However, Spartacus led his men down the other side of the mountain before the soldiers arrived, and came up behind the soldiers. The senate then sent two more legions, which were also defeated by Spartacus and the slaves.

What You Should Know About...

Spartacus

❖ His aide, Crixus, died in battle during the second conflict with Roman soldiers. To avenge Crixus's death, Spartacus forced three hundred prisoners from the legions to battle in pairs to the death, as gladiators did.

❖ When some of the slaves in his group began robbing and destroying villages, Spartacus separated from them and formed another army.

80 BCE **70 BCE** **60 BCE**

72 BCE
Defeats two legions of soldiers sent by the senate in Rome

71 BCE
Dies in battle in southern Italy

The Decline of the Roman Gladiators

Historians believe that the worsening Roman **economy** and the rise of Christianity led to the decline of the Roman gladiators.

The Decline of the Roman Economy

The Roman Empire began to fall into decline during the 300s and 400s CE, and its economy suffered. Putting on gladiatorial games was always extremely costly, but it became more difficult for Rome to fund these events as the economy worsened.

The Rise of Christianity

Most Christians believed that the gladiatorial games were cruel, and many protested against them. In 337 CE, Emperor Constantine made Christianity the Roman Empire's official religion. This allowed Christians who were critical of the games to become more outspoken about their concerns. In 325 CE Emperor Constantine stopped the games, although they continued to be held illegally. In 399 CE Emperor Honorius closed all remaining gladiator schools. In 404 CE he abolished the games after spectators at the Colosseum killed a Christian who tried to stop a gladiator fight.

Many Christians believed that the gladiatorial games went against the teachings of Jesus Christ, who preached kindness and compassion.

Glossary

abolishes   Makes illegal or puts a complete stop to.

amphitheaters   Open-air stadiums with arenas surrounded by seats.

arena   An oval space in the center of an amphitheater.

assassinate   To murder in a surprise attack, usually for political reasons.

awning   A canvas canopy used to protect spectators from the weather.

barracks   Military housing.

chariots   Carriages that essedarii gladiators drove.

citizens   Members of a country or a group of people.

civil rights   Rights that people have, such as the right to vote.

Colosseum   A large amphitheater built in Rome.

crest   The top of a helmet.

decree   An order issued by the emperor.

deserted   Left without giving warning.

economy   The system of producing and distributing resources, business, and money in a society.

elite   The wealthiest or most powerful citizens in a society.

emperor   The ruler of a society, similar to a king.

emulate   Imitate or copy.

Etruscans   People from the region of Etruria, in the country today known as Italy.

excavations   Digging that exposes historical artifacts.

Forum   A public square in Rome where people gathered for political discussion.

freedom   The right to live and work in society without fighting as a gladiator.

inscribed   Carved onto an object.

insubordination   Not obeying authority or breaking the rules.

javelin   A long, pointed spear.

joust   A sport in which men would charge toward each other on horseback with a pointed lance.

legions   Units of the Roman army made up of 3,100 to 6,200 soldiers.

opponents   Gladiators who fought one another in gladiatorial games.

prestigious   Respected and important.

rebel   Person who takes part in a revolt.

revolts   Attempts to start a revolution.

salvaged   Saved from damage.

senate   A group of politicians based in Rome, who met regularly to make decisions on political issues within the Roman Empire.

social classes   Groups of people with different degrees of importance in a society.

spectators   People who watch an event.

strangled   Cut off someone's air supply, usually by squeezing the neck.

tempo   The speed at which a musical piece is played.

trident   A large fork with three prongs, used as a weapon by gladiators.

tyrant   A person who uses power in a cruel manner to make others fear them.

volunteer gladiators   Citizens who chose to become gladiators.

Index